Table of Contents

Introduction

*F*ailure is more likely to come not from technological or financial forces, but from the inability of management to lead and train their employees to truly work as an effective team.

Welcome to our series on *Heart, Soul and Spirit: Bold Strategies for Transforming Your Organization.* This is the first of a series of books discussing the strategies that we propose will increase an organization's productivity and profitability. At The Effectiveness Institute we believe we have developed a powerful new model for transforming organizations. This model states that leaders must possess certain traits–which can be developed–and promote a balance between productivity and satisfaction within their companies, divisions or departments to achieve sustainable levels of higher performance. We believe this is critical because failure is more likely to come not from technological or financial forces, but from the inability of management to lead and train their employees to truly work as an effective team. Heart, Soul and Spirit is dramatically different from the short-term quick-fixes on the training market today. It takes a longer view and mandates focus on issues and practices within the working environment usually ignored by managers.

It also focuses on the bottom-line impact of values such as trust, respect, dignity, integrity and commitment in the workplace.

This book is about the "what's" and "why's" of our model; what is working and why. Each subsequent book will present in-depth strategies, techniques, best practices and extensive detail about how organizations are transforming themselves. It is not necessary to be a CEO or a vice president to apply our principles. The principles are equally effective at all levels of an organization, anywhere there are groups of people working together in some common enterprise. Our interest is in helping you achieve sustainable levels of high performance, and not just another wave of change.

The principles are equally effective at all levels of an organization.

Invitation to Readers

Throughout the development of our model and this
book series we have been introduced to many excep-
tional organizations. We are sure your daily experiences
bring you into contact with such organizations and we
are interested in hearing your stories. We want you to
share your experiences so that we can in turn share
your stories with others. Please send your thoughts to:

Dr. Bill Maynard and Tom Champoux

The Effectiveness Institute, Inc.

2249-152nd Avenue NE

Redmond, Washington 98052

THE CHALLENGE OF COMPETITIVE ADVANTAGE

The pattern for the future has already been established. Those organizations that learn to excel and, more importantly, sustain their levels of excellence will succeed in the new global economy. Those that do not, will likely disappear. Yet as many have discovered, it is much easier to initiate change and improvement than it is to sustain the changes.

Quality improvement, reengineering, rightsizing, world class training, have all resulted in the phenomena of waves of change. Momentum and energy for change builds, the wave sweeps through the organization, and then subsides into an almost unnoticeable lapping at the organization's shore. The changes frequently are short term and rarely result in an increase in a company's ability to achieve and sustain a higher level of performance over time.

In order to truly transform our organizations, to actually achieve and sustain new levels of performance and excellence, it is going to take leaders with heart, soul and spirit. It is going to take leaders with the wisdom and ability to balance the financial and technological forces of the organization with the needs, capabilities and potential of the employees. The employees are

"Excellence is not an accomplishment. It is a spirit, a never-ending process."

Lawrence M. Miller

the people whose collective performance ultimately determines the level of success of the organization. The difficulty of achieving and sustaining excellence is compounded by the nagging drive for short term goals (quarterly earnings), at the expense of long term benefits (sustained excellence). There needs to be a balance; dollars and people working together to achieve greatness.

Productivity and Satisfaction

The performance of a work group or team is a function of the level of productivity achieved by the group and the level of satisfaction experienced by individuals within the group. Together, productivity and satisfaction result in measurable performance. Productivity and satisfaction interact in a way similar to the Eastern concept of yin and yang. Both are necessary, but must be in balance. When the emphasis

In order to truly transform our organizations, to actually achieve and sustain new levels of performance and excellence, it is going to take leaders with heart, soul and spirit.

within the organization is almost exclusively on productivity, performance or the capability of higher levels of performance suffers. If the focus is primarily on the level of satisfaction of employees, again performance suffers.

Our Heart, Soul and Spirit model is based on developing a balance between productivity and satisfaction. This means that in order to achieve higher levels of performance and to sustain these over time, organizations will need a balanced combination of technical/business strategies and strategies focusing on people issues. The strategies we propose help educate individuals to achieve this balance.

BUILDING A
BETTER WORKPLACE

Since 1980, with my partner Tom Champoux and our colleagues at The Effectiveness Institute, we have worked on performance issues and major change strategies with several hundred organizations. Many of the truly productive workplaces we have seen have balance. They demonstrate both exceptionally high levels of performance in terms of output and financial return, and are also places of decency and dignity; places where people treat each other with respect and kindness.

"We want satisfaction from accomplishment and friendships, balanced personal and professional lives, and to have fun in all our endeavors."

Levi Strauss & Company

Unfortunately, many other organizations are skewed. They have not even attempted to achieve a balance between performance and satisfaction. Productivity increases are achieved through forced top-down directives and are seldom sustained for any appreciable length of time. Teamwork is non-existent or an inaccurate description of work groups thrown together and instructed to cooperate. Employee and departmental relations are adversarial and aggressiveness is deemed more valuable than dignity or respect. While this style of organization can still be successful, it robs itself of the full potential of a motivated, team-driven workforce.

When we ask hourly employees about their places of work, 98% tell us they really want to do a good job and also want it to be a better place; more pleasant and fun with less stress and anxiety. They want to be treated with dignity and respect. They are right in their desires. With few exceptions, we have found that a pleasant environment in which people treat each other well and where mutual respect exists, is a more productive place–and healthier. We have worked in places where people treat each other kindly, and in places where people don't. Kind is better. We have been in places where the primary mode of feedback is praise and in those in which it is criticism. Praise is better. When people are treated poorly they become alienated, and when people are habitually criticized they become hostile. They put in their time and look for ways to get even. We are continuously amazed at the insensitivity and shortsightedness of some managers. It is clearly evident that the behavior of managers directly affects the behavior and performance of employees—in productive ways or in counterproductive ways.

The bottom line is profitability. Any change within an organization, division or department needs to result in

*K*ind is better.

*T*he behavior of managers directly affects the behavior and performance of employees–in productive ways or in counter-productive ways.

improved performance. Of equal importance, changes and improvements need to be sustainable, otherwise they become just another wave of change.

Many businesses are now achieving sustained improvement. What follows is a description of the real world experiences and applied lessons of three Effectiveness Institute clients: a four-star hotel, an aerospace company and a chain restaurant organization. Although propriety requires the confidentiality of actual numerical results, these clients were willing to share the process of change they pursued. Each had different motivations for change, ranging from just staying in business to remaining a continuously learning organization. Before we highlight our transformation strategies, we believe it is important for you to see the type of results that are possible when leaders lead with Heart, Soul and Spirit.

A Four Star Hotel

The Summary

The management team of the Stanford Court Hotel in San Francisco was able to turn a very difficult situation, (i.e. red ink, impending strike, alienated workforce), around in less than a year.

The Background

Since its opening and for 18 years, the Stanford Court was owned by one man, a self-styled patriarch. He had created a caring environment. Everyone, including the owner, knew everyone else. They had Christmas parties and picnics, and celebrated births, birthdays and weddings. People took pride in their jobs and helped each other. Many employees had been with the hotel since it opened, and many others had worked there for eight or more years. This level of longevity is unusual in the hotel industry. One of the company legends was about the time a union forced all employees of a group of hotels to strike. The owner of the Stanford Court served coffee to his employees on the picket line.

The Challenge

As is often the case with small, profitable enterprises, the hotel was bought out by a large food conglomerate. A new general manager was sent in; cold, aloof and dictatorial. He brought his own management team. Relationships within the hotel rapidly deteriorated. The union emerged as the necessary protector of the employees. Profits plummeted and then the whole industry went into a tailspin. Hotels had been over-built and travel had declined.

> *T*he employees were angry, hostile and even more alienated.

Two years later the financially troubled hotel was sold again; this time to a hotel chain. Another management team was brought in, causing a fresh round of mistrust between employees and management. Soon the property was facing severe financial problems. The order came down from corporate to down-size. For the first time in the hotel's history, jobs and people were eliminated. The employees were angry, hostile and even more alienated. To compound the situation, negotiations for a new hotel union contract were to begin in three months. The union saw an opportunity for a high visibility coup, and targeted the Stanford Court for a major strike. They were confident that the employees would be eager to support their union's position against management.

The Intervention

Christian Mari was the new general manager, and Collette Boardley the human resources director. They knew that relations with the staff had to be turned around, and quickly. Under their leadership, The Effectiveness Institute initiated a team building process that included all managers and supervisors. But before you build a team you have to find out what the problem is. At Stanford Court the problem wasn't just declining business. That was the result. The major issue was much more fundamental.

We conducted a series of meetings with over 250 employees. After listening to their stories and concerns, the immediate problem became clear. It wasn't money, hours, or benefits. The employees were convinced that the managers didn't care about them. These people were the waiters and waitresses, parking attendants, front desk clerks, housekeepers and bellmen. All of the employees it takes to operate a quality hotel. Here is how they described their perception of the behavior of managers:

> "When we come in to work, they don't say good morning, they don't say anything. Sometimes they don't even look at us. My manager doesn't even know the names of his employees. They talk to us when things are wrong, or tell us when we're doing something wrong, but never say anything if we do things right. We never know what's going on. They never tell us anything. Everything we hear is from rumors. We just want a little respect. Don't they know that we're people too?"

Despite these findings, we knew that Stanford Court had a well intentioned management group. They all

> *The* employees were convinced that the managers didn't care about them.

wanted to do a good job. When we presented them with a summary of our research from the employee meetings there was a variety of predictable reactions. Many of the managers understood immediately. Others wanted to explain or make excuses. But there wasn't time for excuses. The hotel was seriously losing money. It had an alienated and hostile employee staff, and it was targeted for a major strike. In order to turn the situation around, the management team had to have the support of the employees.

The Effectiveness Institute facilitated a series of manager and employee work sessions. They focused on the future and on teamwork. Information on the true state of the hotel was shared. Together the managers and staff created "Vision 2000", their game plan for transformation. We provided them with the tools to surface and evaluate ideas and to mediate future conflicts and problems. But more importantly, we helped them realize their desire to work together as a team to achieve and sustain a higher level of performance which would save their hotel.

The Results

Over the next several months behavior patterns changed significantly. Managers took time to get to know their employees. They scheduled monthly department meetings to keep employees informed of progress and to seek their ideas and help in solving problems. People consciously treated each other with dignity and respect, and morale improved greatly. The executive team held monthly "State of the Business" meetings which were open to all employees. They were told the truth about how things were going. Good and bad. Levels of trust increased between management and the employees. Throughout the hotel there was a significant improvement in individual and department performance. Since the union was no longer able to obtain employee support, there was no strike at the Stanford Court Hotel. Instead, the strike took place at another hotel—literally next door. Through a unified effort, the hotel once again achieved profitability in less than a year. We believe they will be able to sustain it.

An Aerospace Company

The Summary

One manufacturing division decided to take a risk and buck the prevailing corporate culture by creating a caring, team-oriented environment. The mocking comments from other divisions were silenced when their own productivity goals were eclipsed by the "touchy-feely group."

The Background

As in many large manufacturing organizations, the level of *internal* competition within Boeing can be intense and sometimes brutal. Rivalries exist between divisions, and between managers within the divisions. They are part of Boeing's 75-year old culture. Somehow it worked in the past because Boeing, of course, is one of the most successful companies in the world. The global aerospace market is turbulent, and the challenge to Boeing is to not only sustain their success and market share, but continue to find new ways to improve their performance. They have to reduce costs, continuously improve quality and sell airplanes cheaper. To accomplish this will likely require changing many of the old ways of doing things.

> *T*o accomplish this will likely require changing many of the old ways of doing things.

The Challenge

Within the factory that produces 737 and 757 airplanes, some managers are trying to change the culture. John Cornish and Al Stecks are developing a new climate of collaboration, teamwork and high performance in their work groups. Stecks, who at the time was a general production manager reporting to Cornish, started the transformation process several years ago. His organization, like most others, was a "kick butt and take names" workplace. Production was driven purely by the numbers: scheduling, reducing costs of re-work, number of hours on task, etc. Decision making was top down and autocratic. "Do it because I said so" was the norm for supervisor-employee communication. Though the employees worked in a climate of adversity, they usually, but not always were still able to achieve their assigned production goals.

Though he had worked within this culture for 24 years, Stecks decided there must be a better way. He read, he listened and he learned. Then he began with his team of supervisors. "We are going to change the way we treat each other and the way we treat our employees," he told them at a surprise managers meeting. "We are going to learn to work as a team and

We are going to learn to work as a team and you are going to need to develop teamwork with your people. There is no other choice.

you are going to need to develop teamwork with your people. There is no other choice. We've got to learn to communicate and trust each other."

The Intervention

Stecks had the vision, and he knew what the key challenge to achieving it was going to be – "learn to work as a team." Few managers intuitively know how to lead teams. It is an acquired skill. Stecks decided he wasn't going to wait for change to hit his division, he was going to drive it himself. So, for two years, and without formal company approval, The Effectiveness Institute worked with his management group on developing trust, respect and team skills. This was a profound departure from the Boeing corporate culture and not all of his managers wanted to embrace new ways of working. At one point Stecks had to tell a couple of his supervisors, "Change the way you deal with your people or leave." As word got out, Stecks and his supervisors were increasingly criticized by managers in other work areas. They were called the "touchy-feely people", and their work area was called "Disneyland". But they toughed it out. Together, managers and line-level workers began working on a new vision and production plan for their organization.

The Results

The transformation took time, but the results were remarkable. They achieved a clear sense of teamwork and camaraderie within their organization. People became friendly and helped each other. The employee teams developed their own production goals and work plans, and their own standards of performance. While that in and of itself is impressive from an employee satisfaction perspective, the performance improvements which they generated were even more significant. The standards the group set were higher than those of the division. Then they consistently hit or exceeded those goals. In the process they learned to sustain these new levels of both productivity and employee satisfaction.

Though the company has not yet embraced this new culture, John Cornish has. In his work group there are 6 general production managers, 48 supervisors and over 800 employees. Cornish has begun a process of developing collaboration and teamwork throughout his entire organization, and is creating a new climate for how people at all levels work together. Cornish's team has also developed a new vision and "Team Charter", and a plan for its execution.

The following is an excerpt from their vision statement.

Overall Purpose

To provide a teaming environment that nurtures endless development and success for the MBU (Manufacturing Business Unit)

- Employees
- Products
- Customers
- Guiding Principles

We are a caring team committed to common goals based on honesty, trust, respect, open communication and mutual accountability. We promote fun and feel free to express ideas, and recognize the value of individuals and their personal growth. The result is delivering the best product with total customer satisfaction.

The changes in managers and supervisors have been dramatic. The following are some of their words as they described where they see themselves now:

"This has been the best experience I've had in all my years at our company. The way this group teamed and worked together was extraordinary. I am looking forward to this team working together and growing as a cross-functional team".

"We have begun a long journey. One that has been needed/required for years. I believe we have all the right people to make this journey and to end up as winners at the end, as long as we stay on the path and stay with the journey. I feel good about what we are doing. I am excited to be a part of the team. I look forward to where we are going."

"This process has increased my optimism about the future of our organization and our company in general. I believe that we have the opportunity to affect real change. I believe we can be world class. I believe we hold the future in our hands to affect everything around us. I no longer feel as alone."

It is too soon to know what the long term results will be, or even if the company can tolerate such dramatic internal change. If they do, there will be a significant change in how they build airplanes.

A Chain Restaurant Company

The Summary

The Harman Management Corporation, located in Los Altos, California is the largest franchisee of Kentucky Fried Chicken. They currently have 265 stores and are growing at a controlled rate of 5-8 new stores per year. The company clearly understands the power of caring management and relies on it to achieve performance standards superior to those within their industry.

The Background

Pete Harman joined up with Colonel Sanders in 1952, and formed what is now KFC. At age 75, Harman is still active in the daily business. He and his team have built one of the most profitable chain restaurant organizations. But it is the "Harman way" that really makes them different in a highly competitive and difficult industry. "We choose intelligent people and all promotions are from within," states Jackie Trujillo, recently appointed as CEO. "We expect a lot from our people, and want them to be the best they can be." From the very beginning, Pete Harman created a place where people care about each other. According to Trujillo, "You can have a philosophy, but what good is it if it isn't implemented?" Trujillo has worked with Harman since she was 16 years old.

> *Y*ou can have a philosophy, but what good is it if it isn't implemented?

Though the management team remains close to their people, the size of the company has resulted in a reliance on the 26 district managers to implement the Harman philosophy with over 5500 employees. Each district manager supervises ten stores, and is expected to personally know each employee. In fact, the number one criteria for the selection of district managers is that

they really care about their people, and will do everything they can to help them succeed. "It wasn't always
like that," says Trujillo. "At one time we chose them
for results only, and got ourselves in trouble. We want
them to do their job with love and concern at all times.
The caring shouldn't stop just because a manager or
employee isn't doing well. Anybody can care when
people are doing everything right."

It is the Harman philosophy to "share with employees,
and it will all come back to you." They teach their
young managers and assistant managers how to be
business people. After working successfully as a relief
manager for a year, he or she can begin buying stock in
the company. Once a manager, they can purchase up to
30% ownership in their store (40% if a husband-wife
team). In some cases Harman has even guaranteed a
loan with a bank to help the manager get started. "We
want each of them to become financially independent
and determine his or her own destiny," says Harman.

*All managers
are expected to become
highly active within
their communities.*

All managers are expected to become highly active
within their communities. Harman believes "it makes
for better people." Managers are heavily involved in
D.A.R.E. programs, as well as chambers of commerce

and merchant associations. The majority of employees are high school students, and it is not unusual to find KFC managers attending and celebrating the graduation activities of their people.

Harman Management provides support to scholarship funds, Children's Hospital and other community organizations. In 1993 they "adopted" an Oakland inner-city high school. The intent was to provide unencumbered support to the principal, staff and students for improving student self-esteem, academic achievement and safety. This too, is a reflection of the deep commitment Harman has to the community. "We don't realize the importance we play in other people's lives," he says. "We have a great responsibility to help others succeed. I take it very personally. I want our people and other people to be better; to be happier."

A major highlight for managers, assistant managers and their spouses is attending one of the two conventions held each year, usually in San Diego and Hawaii. These are six-day, all expense paid trips to major resorts for nearly 800 people. There are events designed for people to enjoy each other and attend informative business meetings. They serve as a potent symbol of the Harman company's successful balance between productivity and satisfaction.

The Results

By all standards, Harman Management Corporation is a very successful company. Pete Harman has a firm belief that "the more you give to people, the more you get back". It comes back to the company in many forms: financial success, longevity, personal growth and satisfaction for employees. Harman's annual sales exceed $220 million, and their revenues run about 20% above the industry averages. The annual turnover rate at the management level runs 14% in an industry that frequently has a 50-100% turnover rate. Employee turnover is less than half of the industry average. As one manager stated, "all of these factors wouldn't have much punch at all if it weren't for the genuine caring and concern of Pete Harman and Jackie Trujillo. They really care about the success of their people."

Managing with Heart, Soul and Spirit

Each of these case studies highlighted companies at different stages of transformational change. The Stanford Court Hotel had to achieve a complete turnaround in behavior and performance to survive. John Cornish's manufacturing group at Boeing needed assistance in creating a new culture that was capable of reaching higher levels of performance. At KFC, it was all about staying smart and sustaining the level of success they had earned as a caring, productive workforce. The Effectiveness Institute is proud to have assisted these talented managers and companies in leading with Heart, Soul and Spirit.

But what is the source of our philosophy? What circumstances allowed these strategies to be formed and tested? The following is a brief history of our experience. It also summarizes the lessons we have learned, which when applied to the workplace, profoundly improves performance over time.

THE FOUNDATION OF OUR EXPERIENCE

"In organizations, real power and energy is generated through relationships. The patterns of relationships and the capacities to form them are more important than tasks, functions, roles and positions."

Margaret Wheatley,

Leadership and the

New Science

Originally Tom and I came from the field of public education; actually inner-city high schools. What we learned about changing hostile high school situations has served us well in dealing with business challenges. There is no more difficult environment to manage than that of an inner-city school. It is the ultimate environment of competition: competition for grades in the classroom and for scholarships, for self importance and popularity, for clique (or gang) superiority, and there is intense recruiting and athletic competition. For the students there is a continuous contest resulting in winners and losers, and haves and have-nots. For the staff of a high school, there is severe competition for scarce resources. Power struggles spring up between department heads and between departments. Polarization and coalitions exist: teachers against administrators, administrators against teachers, and union against management. There are some teachers and administrators who just do not like kids. To compound the management difficulty, it is nearly impossible to terminate poorly performing educators, so they are passed from one school to another bringing their problems with them.

We learned that despite the extreme difficulties,we could make a dramatic improvement in levels of performance. At the high school we measured results and performance outcomes in grade points, the percentage of students going to college, absentee and drop-out rates and standardized test scores. Businesses measure theirs in terms of ratios, bottom-line profits and stock values. Yet the dynamics of motivation and performance within these vastly different kinds of organizations are the same. Businesses can learn from successful schools and schools can learn from successful businesses.

Riots to Results

In 1971 I was appointed principal of Cleveland High School in Seattle, Washington. Cleveland was an inner-city high school experiencing traumatic times. I was the sixth principal in nine years. In my meeting with the school superintendent I was given only one instruction; "Bill, don't have a riot." Cleveland was a small school with a loser image and in recent years had become a racial hot spot continuously on the brink of eruption.

> *There is no more difficult environment to manage than that of an inner-city school. It is the ultimate environment of competition.*

> *It was a leadership and management nightmare.*

The staff was dealing with escalating racial problems, anti-war demonstrations, drugs and weapons. None of us were trained for nor had any experience in dealing with the things that were happening. It was a leadership and management nightmare.

The enrollment in Cleveland High was nearly 80% minority students, and was composed of every different ethnic group living in our city. There was a great deal of tension and hostility among the staff as well as among the students. Fights broke out almost daily. Of the city's twelve high schools, Cleveland had the highest drop-out rate, the highest absentee rate, the highest suspension rate and the highest number of incidents of violence and vandalism.

The loser image was compounded by a run down, dreary old building, and by athletic teams that were perpetually trounced on by the other schools.

Keeping a lid on the place was all we could manage during the first school year. Little changed, except for perhaps one thing; some staff members with true heart and soul stepped forward. Several of us began developing trust in one another and in building our relationships. Emmett Kinkade, Jim Sampson and

Tom Champoux were instrumental in initiating this subtle change. This core group then began developing trust and building relationships with students of all the different ethnic groups.

Whereas most math teachers taught only their subject matter, Emmett taught kids. He built relationships with them, and then taught math. I learned from Emmett that teaching from the heart was more important than teaching from the head. Every student whose heart he touched, regardless of their ability, had a high probability of succeeding in Emmett's class. He knew how to get maximum performance out of his people.

Jim Sampson was not a typical P.E. teacher or football coach. Rather than an attitude of "my way is the only way," his approach was to do whatever it took to help students learn and succeed. Jim would experiment with new programs and strategies, while others were entrenched in their old ways of doing things.

> *Teaching from the heart was more important than teaching from the head.*

Tom Champoux's job was teaching language arts, but he too was a heart person. Tom had an unconditional love for all of his students and consistently treated them with respect and dignity. In turn, the kids loved Tom and worked hard to perform well in his classes.

Tom was a coach, a counselor and a friend as well as their teacher. He also became one of the most important staff leaders in the school.

The second year was different. We learned that dramatic change can occur almost instantaneously, and be sustained. From a staff of over 70, it was the support and leadership of these three that became the catalyst for creating a new kind of school. In organizational change, a few people can make a big difference.

Rapid change requires rapid learning. From the beginning it was clear that our whole society had changed. We were continuously confronted with the conflict between the old ways of doing things and the new challenges brought on by change. The old ways simply didn't work anymore. To survive, we had to do things differently but we had no knowledge, skills or frame of reference to help us understand what was happening or what to do. We did make a key observation. When what you are doing isn't working, you tend to do more of the same and with greater intensity. We would fall back on the old, comfortable ways thinking they would work again. But life never returns to the way things were.

*W*hen what you are doing isn't working, you tend to do more of the same and with greater intensity.

We had to learn new ways of doing things in a very short time frame. This required innovation, experimentation, breaking old barriers and dealing with tremendous resistance to change. In fact, the greater the need for change, the greater the resistance. No matter how difficult that is, it is the only way to break out of old comfort zones. We found that as the rate of change increases, so too must the rate of learning. It is not just a matter of succeeding, it may be the only way to survive.

The dramatic turning point occurred early that fall. Typically, the football team had lost their first two games and were trying to prepare for the third. In fact, in five years Cleveland had won only three games. A group of students asked the administrators if they could have a pep assembly prior to the game. They didn't tell us that their request had already been turned down by a faculty committee. We did know that the previous administrators had banned assemblies and dances for fear of a riot. Just before the assembly the students told us they had not been able to find anyone to give a pep speech. No one would come out to

> *We* found that as the rate of change increases, so too must the rate of learning.

Cleveland High, so they asked me, the principal, to make the talk. This scared the heck out of all of us. If I lost control at the assembly we would definitely have a difficult situation on our hands.

There were about 900 rather somber students sitting in the gym expecting something, but not sure what. They all sat within their ethnic groups. The staff members who had been developing relationships with the students were sitting with them in the stands before the assembly. The rest of the staff was not there. I was very scared and could think of only three things to say. One was about caring and reaching out and helping each other. The second was that we were in this together and we needed to reach out to each other across the ethnic boundaries. The third was about pride; having pride in ourselves, pride in our ethnicity and pride in our school which had the greatest diversity and potential in the city. In closing I asked them, "Do you have pride?" Their first response was a rather quiet "yes," so I asked the question again. "Do you have pride?" Their next response overwhelmed all of us. Several students yelled back at me, "Yeah, we've got pride!" Then it started. A small group began chanting, "We've got pride! We've got pride!" Then another group started chanting, then another, and within a few seconds the entire assembly was standing and chanting, "WE'VE GOT PRIDE!"

In retrospect, I believe that was the moment when the tide changed. Over the next several weeks we watched the barriers break down. The students painted "WE'VE GOT PRIDE" on the wall in the main hall. This became our vision and eventually resulted in permanent changes in both behavior and performance in our school.

That year our football team had its first non-losing season in 33 years. Our coach was chosen "Coach of the Year" for winning four games. He won the honor again the following year for getting our team into the championship playoffs. Our baseball team won the city championship. The following year our basketball team placed third in the state and then won back-to-back state championships over the next two years. But athletics was only a small part of the important changes that took place at Cleveland. Relationships developed between students, and between staff and students. As the levels of trust and respect increased, so too did the level of pride they took in themselves and in their school.

A small group began chanting, "We've got pride! We've got pride!" Then another group started chanting, then another, and within a few seconds the entire assembly was standing and chanting, "WE'VE GOT PRIDE!"

> *We were finding ways for creating a new climate within our school—a climate of heart, soul, and spirit.*

We began involving students from all grades on problem solving and decision making teams with staff members who wanted to participate. Collaboration and teamwork became one of our primary vehicles for change. Life-skills courses were added, curricula changed, teaching methods improved, staff behavior towards students was addressed, values were stressed and we improved the ways we evaluated both student and staff performance. We were finding ways for creating a new climate within our school—a climate of heart, soul, and spirit. As an administrative team we came to view our job as that of doing everything we could to help every student succeed.

During the next few years we moved from having the highest absentee rate in the city to the lowest. We also dropped from the highest rate of suspensions and drop-outs to the lowest. Instead of graffiti, our halls were decorated with drawings of eagles (our mascot), painted by the students. The main hall was titled "The Hall Of Eagles," and became a news story on national television. Grade points started climbing, and more students began enrolling in post high school education programs.

It became clear that five values had emerged as driving forces for defining our new culture at Cleveland. Those values were trust, respect, dignity, integrity and commitment. We have since found the impact of these values to be the same in all organizations.

Lessons Learned

It seems every company wants commitment from its employees, but in our experience there is rarely commitment without trust and respect. We found that when students were treated with respect and dignity, their behavior improved and so did our relationships with them. As their relationships with each other improved, so too did their self respect and sense of dignity. We now know that all of these experiences contributed to improvements in performance. Trust, respect and dignity have the same effect in the workplace.

The integrity of leaders is fundamental to building a high performance organization. We had to be honest with each other and especially with the students. We had to consistently do what we said we would do, even when students didn't like it. It was paramount that our

> *The* integrity of leaders is fundamental to building a high performance organization.

behavior match our words; that we "walk our talk." When we did this, students perceived us to be credible and authentic. To them our authenticity determined whether or not we were trustworthy.

In our experience, the perceived authenticity and integrity of leaders has a direct effect on the willingness of people to pull together in difficult times. Without integrity there will be no trust and respect, and relationships will be, at best, superficial.

> *C*ontrol, force and fear, the usual tools for transformation, could not change student behavior and performance, but Heart, Soul and Spirit did.

The true source of heart, soul and spirit was really within the students themselves. It had been squelched for nearly two decades. Their internal beliefs had been that they were second class people in a second class school. They were losers. Either they conformed to the rules and the established culture, or they were terminated. Many simply quit. The leaders and teachers (middle managers) perpetuated a system that had not worked for many years. The performance of this organization was far below mediocrity. Control, force and fear, the usual tools for transformation, could not change student behavior and performance, but Heart, Soul and Spirit did.

HEART, SOUL AND SPIRIT

Over the last sixteen years, The Effectiveness Institute has worked with very large organizations with over 100,000 employees, and organizations with fewer than a hundred employees. Each organization has gone through significant change. Though the changes were unique to each company, the dynamics were almost always the same. They had lost market share, or were worried about it. Revenues were down. They were down-sizing, re-engineering or trying to improve quality. Where they were was not where they needed to be in order to compete in a global economy. The way they used to do things did not seem to work anymore. These organizations all experienced a great deal of internal disharmony and chaos. Even though it was critical that they collaborate, many people did not like each other and did not work well together. The rivalry between internal groups turned vicious.

The "kids" in these organizations are older, have more finely honed defenses and more deeply embedded beliefs and behavior patterns. However, the dynamics within the organizations were the same as those we first experienced in schools.

Matters of the Heart

The heart of an organization is like the heart of an individual. It is the source of energy and strength, compassion and courage. The organization's heart is a mirror of the collective hearts of its leaders. Some organizations have no heart. This is self-limiting and sad, but true. Though some of them are profitable, they create their own barriers and frequently are unpleasant places to work.

Notice that there are so many phrases about heart. Have a heart...deep in our hearts we know the truth... his heart wasn't in it...it warms my heart...follow your heart...the heartbeat of America.

The heart is the center of all that is good, or can be good about an organization. The heart pumps the life blood of the organization. In a heart organization the leaders are interested in hiring the whole person, not just a body. Caring is recognized as a powerful force, and dignity, morale, trust and playing on the same team are important. This is critical because significant results are achieved through people building the best together.

> The heart of an organization is like the heart of an individual. It is the source of energy and strength, compassion and courage.

In working with organizations, we have learned to follow a simple path. When we have strayed from the path, the results of our work have been less successful, or we have failed to accomplish what we had intended. Before agreeing to work with a client, we try to determine if the leader has heart. If the answer is no, we are resistant to doing the work until the heart issue is addressed.

Most leaders have been selected and trained as head people, not heart people. So, most organizations are still head organizations, and being rational and logical is what's important. Employees are hired to do a job. Numbers, measurements, charts and graphs drive decisions; particularly as they relate to bottom line results and stock price. People issues are either not viewed as important, or they are addressed only if there is time, which usually means not at all. If they are addressed, it is because of an effort to improve numbers (the head), rather than relationships (the heart).

> *M*ost leaders have been selected and trained as head people, not heart people. So, most organizations are still head organizations, and being rational and logical is what's important.

It does not always need to be a choice between head decisions and heart decisions. An organization that balances head decisions and heart decisions has a far greater potential for achieving and sustaining success than an organization that doesn't have heart.

When leaders and employees come from the heart, their behavior is different. They find new depths of energy and courage to deal with adversity, to innovate and to do whatever it takes to make the right things happen.

Matters of the Soul

Soul is about the belief in something good; something powerful; something with deep meaning. Soul is the vital core and the vital force from which emanates a deeper meaning about work and about life. Soul lets us know there is more that is important than just getting up, going to work and going home. There is more than a paycheck, a bonus, or a percentage increase in after-tax profits.

In our soul we know we are valuable human beings and there is an important purpose and meaning to life. Work must play a part in this purpose. We cannot pretend that work has no impact on us, our co-workers, or our communities. An organization without soul is a workplace for the dead. Sometimes leaders sell their soul and the soul of their organization in order to fulfill some immediate short term or personal gain. Caring and decency disappear and this limits the life expectancy of the organization.

> Soul is the vital core and the vital force from which emanates a deeper meaning about work and about life.

In an organization with soul, people know their work is more than just a job. They know their presence makes a difference, and that every individual is important. The success of the company is important... and people develop a passion for producing the best they possibly can.

Matters of Spirit

Spirit is the expression of the passion that comes from loyalty, dedication, belief and commitment. It's about school spirit and team spirit. The kids would stand and scream in unison, "We've got spirit; yes we do! We've got spirit; how about you?" They would celebrate when we won, and cry together when we lost. The participants in the stands were as important as the players on the field. Why should we think our work life is any different? We could all benefit from a passion for winning, and celebrating together. The success of every individual, regardless of position, is vital to the success of the organization.

> *We* could all benefit from a passion for winning, and celebrating together.

Spirit has a lot to do with loyalty and commitment. When we "catch the spirit" we can feel the energy. We want to be a part of it. We want to contribute, to help the team win, to do whatever it takes to make it happen. It feels good. It feels right. We like being there because it's energizing and we know we are making a difference. It is not about money, it is about winning together. It touches our heart and adds meaning to our soul. We get stronger and healthier and performance improves dramatically.

Spirit is the vitality of an organization. It is the positive energy that connects us all to the feeling of "WE." We are in this together because we want to be, and we can do it!

> *S*pirit is the vitality of an organization. It is the positive energy that connects us all to the feeling of "WE." We are in this together because we want to be, and we can do it!

PRINCIPLES OF TRANSFORMATION

"Every organization must be prepared to abandon everything it does to survive in the future."

Peter Drucker

In business there are no guarantees of success. But at The Effectiveness Institute we have developed a set of transformational principles that get results. No matter what type of organization, department or workgroup you manage, there are specific dynamics you will have to deal with to initiate and sustain change. Here are some important principles we have learned about leadership and transformation.

1 *Heart, soul and spirit are very powerful and dynamic forces within organizations.* When they are present, people tend to have better relationships, are more adaptable to change and adversity, are more innovative and supportive, and have more fun. We need to bring heart, soul and spirit into our organizations.

2 *The values of Trust, Respect, Dignity, Integrity and Commitment are cornerstones for building great organizations.* These are the values upon which relationships are built. We have found most leaders of organizations want, and usually demand, loyalty and commitment from employees. Yet in our experience, there can be little loyalty or commitment without trust, respect and dignity.

People tend to have difficulty defining trust. We have learned that trust is very tentative, that it frequently takes a long time to develop, yet can be destroyed in an instant. Of the several variables that affect trust, one has by far the greatest impact. It is that you care. Love and caring are the most powerful of human emotions in terms of their positive effect on trust in relationships. This is just as true in the workplace as it is in our other relationships.

3 *Creating a climate of caring greatly enhances the heart, soul and spirit of an organization.* A climate of caring facilitates relationships and learning. Individuals who feel cared about and appreciated tend to risk more and produce more. This results in higher levels of group performance and a greater sense of team.

We first became aware of the power of caring in our high school. Teachers who cared about the students had by far a more positive relationship with them, and a more positive effect on their performance than those who did not seem to care. Students would change their behavior, work harder, frequently have better relationships with other students, and earn better grades in these classes. Many students were so deeply

Love and caring are the most powerful of human emotions in terms of their positive effect on trust in relationships. This is just as true in the workplace as it is in our other relationships.

> *T*hose leaders who demonstrate a high degree of caring for their employees and create a work climate within which people appreciate and care about each other, experience vastly greater performance results than those who create a climate of judgment and undue criticism.

touched by their relationship with caring teachers or administrators that years later they still tell of the experience they had and how it changed their lives.

From the research and from our own experience we have learned an interesting principle regarding leaders in businesses and organizations. Those leaders who demonstrate a high degree of caring for their employees and create a work climate within which people appreciate and care about each other, experience vastly greater performance results than those who create a climate of judgment and undue criticism. (But there seems to be a lot more of the latter.)

4 *Building a collaborative organization and developing effective teamwork at all levels is paramount to sustaining innovation and higher levels of performance.* People at all levels must learn to work as either team leaders or team participants. This means that regardless of the situation, the right group of employees could be pulled together from throughout the organization, and quickly function as a highly effective and responsive team. This is what collaboration around a common goal is all about—sharing talents, skills and resources with others to accomplish the goal in spite of adversity and obstacles. And not worrying about who gets the credit.

Teamwork is one of the most powerful vehicles available for innovation and transformation. Yet true teamwork is difficult to achieve. Most frequently, people are simply placed into groups and called a team. Effective teamwork requires developing:

- high levels of trust,
- high levels of respect,
- commitment to a common vision, and
- mutual responsibility and accountability.

Without these, groups of individuals are simply work groups rather than teams. Work groups frequently do not perform well over time and often become dysfunctional. Internal rivalries destroy trust, respect and collaboration. Win-lose competition within the organization results in polarization and sabotage. Energy is expended on blaming, defending and justifying rather than on working together to build the best possible organization.

> *W*in-lose competition within the organization results in polarization and sabotage.

> *The leader
> determines the
> climate—good or bad—of
> his or her organization,
> team or work group.
> And that climate
> directly impacts the
> level of performance
> of all the people.*

5 *The leader is the most significant single factor in determining the climate of the organization, and the climate directly impacts the level of performance and success of people within an organization.* Good leaders lead by example, influence and collaboration. Poor ones lead by intimidation, or by default. The leader determines the climate—good or bad—of his or her organization, team or work group. And that climate directly impacts the level of performance of all the people.

In working with people from the hourly level to executives and CEO's, we have been intrigued by the behavior of the leaders and their impact on people and performance. We found individuals at all levels who were not only effective, but were also inspiring. It wasn't that the leaders were necessarily charismatic. Instead, they most frequently were described by others as authentic. They were real. They came from the heart and they achieved results.

We refer to them as *Inspired Leaders* and are convinced that this is the type of leadership that organizations need to develop today. We have determined that there are four criteria for inspired leaders:

- they have a vision for their organization or team,
- they have a passion for what they are doing,
- they are people of integrity, and
- they have the courage to act, even when it is contrary to the culture. They do what they think is the right thing to do for their people as well as for the company and community.

6 *In order to sustain success over time, the focus needs to be on continuous and rapid learning at all levels of the organization.* Fads of the year and waves of change have not been successful in sustaining success. In many cases, they have left a bad taste of cynicism in the mouths of those who have been "trained."

In addition to Peter Senge's work (The Fifth Discipline) on learning organizations, we like the recent research of Calhoun Wick and David Ulrich. They have been studying the learning speed of organizations and the

> *Foster a climate of lifelong learning and development.*

ability to foster a climate of lifelong learning and development. Their emphasis is on the development of the capabilities of people at all levels as instrumental to the organization's ability to sustain success.

7 *Organizations which promote worthy values and ethics have a far greater probability of sustaining long term success than those that do not.* We have also learned the difference between ethical issues, where it is clear that one way is right and the other wrong, and ethical dilemmas, where there is no clear answer.

> *I*t costs very little to develop clear values and ethical processes, and to teach people to handle the delicate balances and difficult choices.

In business today, leaders are constantly faced with delicate balance decisions between what is right for the customer and what is good for the company; or between the needs of the employees and the need to increase profitability and shareholder return.

We have come to realize the great significance of values and ethics to an organization's ability to sustain success. It costs very little to develop clear values and ethical processes, and to teach people to handle the delicate balances and difficult choices. The cost of lost trust, reduced credibility, lost resources and damaged relationships is however, staggering.

FIVE BOLD STRATEGIES FOR TRANSFORMING YOUR ORGANIZATION

"Whatever you can do, or dream you can...begin it. Boldness has genius, power and magic in it."

Goethe

Many of our client organizations are stuck in their cultures; old behavior patterns and old ways of doing things. For the most part, their leaders have not been trained in transformation strategies or in managing people through change. They implement quality improvement, teamwork, world class training and then they re-engineer. *Waves of change.* They want to become more innovative and adaptable, knowing it is the only way they can maintain success or perhaps even survive. *More waves of change.*

They are right in principle, but frequently wrong in how they execute. Managers and supervisors want something to help transform their organizations. They know that what they are doing is not working. Unfortunately, there is a strong tendency to respond to quick fixes and to shift training resources to the latest fad influential leaders are currently supporting. Compounding the impact, almost all learning and training is focused on either technical or financial skills and strategies, and very little in developing people skills. The U.S. Chamber of Commerce reports that 85-90% of all training dollars spent are on technical skills training. Yet, on-line managers report that 87-95% of all the problems they face are not technical, but people problems.

We have been researching and promoting new ways of balancing the technical and financial needs of the organization with the needs of people, in creating successful organizational change. From our foundational experiences at Cleveland, and our extensive work as consultants with many organizations dealing with change, we have developed five strategies for transformation. They succinctly summarize the many lessons and observations we have discussed so far. In each case, the strategy targets an activity or condition that can bring about sustained levels of higher performance. If change cannot be sustained within an organization, it is not really a transformation.

> *If* change cannot be sustained within an organization, it is not really a transformation.

Strategy One—Create a Climate of Caring

"A business can never have too many customers, too many capital assets, or too much decency."
Theodore Leavitt, editor
Harvard Business Review

Leavitt's comment about decency goes to the heart of the most important key for transformation and sustaining success. A caring organization is more healthy, innovative, fun and profitable.

Strategy Two—Build a Collaborative Organization

> "…there is no contest between the company that buys the grudging compliance of its work force and the company that enjoys the enterprising participation of its employees."
>
> Ricardo Sempler
> *Maverick: The Success Story Behind the World's Most Unusual Workplace*

A collaborative organization is one in which *all* employees work together, share knowledge, skills and resources, and accept mutual responsibility for the success of the organization. The prevailing attitude is, "we're in this together, and we need each other in order to win." Teamwork at all levels is promoted, and destructive internal rivalries are eliminated.

Strategy Three—Develop Inspired Leadership

> "The quality of leadership more than any other single factor, determines the success or failure of an organization."
>
> Fred Fiedler
> Martin Chemers
> *Improving Leadership Effectiveness*

◆ *Inspirare* is a Latin verb for "breathe life into". This is exactly what inspired leaders do for their people. They have a vision for their organization or team. They have a passion for what they are doing. They are people of integrity. They have the courage to act, to decide boldly, even if it is contrary to company culture. Inspired leaders do what they think is right for their people as well as for their company and community. They bring heart, soul and spirit to their workplace. We believe this type of leadership can be developed at all levels of an organization.

Strategy Four—Focus on Continuous Learning

"Learning speed is the rate at which an organization acquires and puts into action the knowledge and capabilities that create competitive advantage and improved business results."

Calhoun Wick
David Ulrich
Racing on the Learning Curve

Adaptability, the ability to "turn on a dime," and innovation are essential to an organization's future success. Whatever the vision, people must be provided with the knowledge and skills necessary to accomplish it. Vision without execution is failure. Through training, and through continuously learning to learn faster, organizations increase their competitive advantage and business results.

Strategy Five—Promote Worthy Values

"In the business environment your values are reflected in
three distinct kinds of decisions: How you spend money,
how you use your time, and how you treat other people."
John Buller
*Survival Guide for
Bureaucratic Warriors*

The rate of change, plus the number and kind of
decisions managers must make, pushes the limits of
what is "right" versus what people sometimes have
to do to "get things done." For many organizations,
success will be determined by managing this delicate
balance and respecting the difficult choices their
people make as they attempt to "do the right thing."
Ethics and values are about "decency," doing what is
good for the organization and what is right for the
customers and the employees.

Our "Bold Strategies" model is based on developing a
balance between productivity and satisfaction. This
means that in order to achieve high levels of perfor-

mance and to sustain these over time, organizations
will need a balanced combination of technical/business
strategies, and strategies focusing on people issues.
The strategies we propose help educate individuals to
achieve this balance.

Epilogue

This book is the first in our series. We hope that it has provided an understanding of how our experiences have generated the principles that we use in our own organization and with our clients. Subsequent books will describe the five transformation strategies in detail, with techniques and examples we have collected from numerous clients in business and industry.

Whatever your vision, share it with your people. Provide them with the knowledge and skills necessary to achieve this vision. Many leaders forget to do one or the other. We think you should have your people read this book. At the very least, you will be able to discuss with them those things that are important to you. Remember, transformation is a journey, not an event. For those who want to be the best, there is no end, just new beginnings.

> Transformation is a journey, not an event. For those who want to be the best, there is no end, just new beginnings.

ORDERING ADDITIONAL COPIES
OF HEART, SOUL AND SPIRIT

*I*t is our hope that you are now inspired to begin transforming your organization. Other members of your team or company could benefit from reading *Heart, Soul and Spirit*. See the order form on the reverse side for details on obtaining volume discounts for ordering multiple copies.

If you realize you need assistance in improving the balance of productivity and satisfaction in your organization, consider The Effectiveness Institute. Our services range from training sessions to customized consulting to keynote addresses. Let us help you achieve a higher level of sustained excellence.

The Effectiveness Institute, Inc.
2249 152nd Avenue N.E.
Redmond, Washington 98052

Toll Free	(800) 805-8654
Telephone	(206) 641-7620
Facsimile	(206) 747-0439
E-Mail Address	effinst@aol.com

Order Form

☐ **Yes!** I'd like to order *"Heart, Soul & Spirit"* and share with my team the proven strategies for transforming our organization.

To order, mail in this form to The Effectiveness Institute. For immediate service call: **1-800-805-8654** or fax to (206) 747-0439.

_____
Name

_____
Title

_____
Organization

(___) _____ (___) _____
Phone   Fax

_____
Mailing Address (street, city, state, zip & country)

_____
Purchase Order Number (if necessary)

Check Method of Payment: ☐ Check   ☐ MasterCard   ☐ Visa
Make check payable to: The Effectiveness Institute, Inc.

_____
Credit Card Account Number   Expiration Date

_____
Signature

Quantity Category	No. of Copies	Price (each)	Total Book Cost
1-99	_____	$9.99	_____
100-999	_____	$8.99	_____
1,000+	_____	$7.99	_____

Shipping and Handling:

(First Class Mail) 1 Book $2.25
2-5 Books (7-10 Days) $4.50
6-10 Books (7-10 Days) $9.00
UPS 11-100 Books (7-10 Days) $18.00
UPS 11-100 Books (Next Day Delivery) $36.00
Over 100 Books, call for specific charges.

Shipping & Handling *(see box)* _____

WA residents
add 8.2% sales tax _____

Total Cost _____

Separate and mail completed form to:

The Effectiveness Institute, Inc., 2249 152nd Avenue N.E., Redmond, WA 98052
(800) 805-8654 • (206) 641-7620 • Fax (206) 747-0439